MEDICAL PLANNER AND JOURNAL (CUSTOMIZED)

MEDICAL PLANNER AND JOURNAL (CUSTOMIZED) FOR GYNECOLOGIST.

REYS N JOURNAL

Dedicated to the best sister/doctor. You are the most hardworking person I've ever seen In my life. Don't let anyone bring you down. Forever my inspiration.

Contents

Contents